D1213704

SHELLS BY A STREAM

Books by Edmund Blunden

POEMS, 1930–1940
THOMAS HARDY

SHELLS BY A STREAM

New Poems

by

EDMUND BLUNDEN

LONDON
MACMILLAN & CO. LTD
1944

PRINTED IN GREAT BRITAIN
BY R. & R. CLARK, LIMITED, EDINBURGH

To

CLAIRE

WITH DEVOTION

CONTENTS

THE HOME OF POETRY

WILLING to give whatever art I know
To some new theme or old one newly springing,
I hear fresh hours appeal, I mark the flow
Of daring wits ; they promise well. I go
Where older friends are singing.

It is not mine to choose ; the deeper call
Is master yet. The child is that they made him.
His eyes, his voice, his mien and walk are all
Out of his jurisdiction. Life arrayed him,
And life will weave his pall.

A thousand ways I travelled, and I heard
A thousand ways of reasoning and regarding ;
And sometime hoped to find some thought and word
Which might swell my estate — a hope deferred,
Now noted for discarding.

So mighty is the motherhood of sense,
The poetry of time before the yearning
For poetry took form ! The narrow fence
Of first things is song's liberty. Returning,
I hail magnificence.

SHELLS BY A STREAM

LEISURELY over lea and grove and stream
The New-Year afternoon moved, my example :
Leisurely I sought out old friends. The oak
Whose crown had been our summer roof when still

Brothers and sisters now thrown far apart
Sat to one loaf, still domed that peaceful place.
The same brook hurried under which had swirled
Uncountable petals, berries, sprigs and leaves
Down to the deep even since we watched it then.
And this our brook had spread its usual sands
In smooth wave-sculptures footing its clift walls,
Thereon again leaving, as children leave
Some of their toys, a twinned shell here and there,
Gleaming without the sun's help, that veiled hour,
In orient honours. Loving to see these shells,
I caught a whispering in the wakening wind :
" Brief is the life of these brook-jewels, bright
Their transience, and of this birth only ; here
On puny reefs they glisten sometimes, here
For a day or so may stay to show what comes
Without display, and without jealous guard,
When purling streams are sent through marl and clay.
These now are miniatures of heaven's blue cup
With live light damascened ; and these existed
That slowest humblest water-serfs might work
Like harvesters in singlets ; never knowing
What wonder they half made and half received,
Yet sensible of the rightness of their world."

OCTOBER COMES

I HEARD the graybird bathing in the rill,
And fluttering his wings dry within thorn boughs
Which all embowered the rill ; with tiny bill
The robin on red-berried spray bade rouse

One whom I could not see, a field away ;
I heard the passing girl to her young man say,
" O look, there's a buttercup " ; for Autumn brought
them still.

Upon my hand the fly so small that sight
Hardly could shape him settled, quested, flew ;
Above me crowns of cloud and thrones of light
Moved with the minutes, and the season's blue,
Autumn's soft raiment, veiled some forms of dream
Which I yet reverence ; once more to my stream
The clear forget-me-not drew my eyes ; the vole watched
too.

He watched, and ate his chosen leaf ; well-furred,
Well-fed he felt for water, winter, all.
Whoever else came by, midge, moth or bird,
The time was easy, nor did one leaf fall
From willow or elm that hour, though millions
glowed
With such wild flame as evening shot abroad
To warn that even this calm was not perpetual.

WHAT IS WINTER ?

THE haze upon the meadow
Denies the dying year,
For the sun's within it, something bridal
Is more than dreaming here.
There is no end, no severance,
No moment of deliverance,

No quietus made,
Though quiet abounds and deliverance moves
In that sunny shade.

What is winter ? a word,
A figure, a clever guess.
That time-word does not answer to
This drowsy wakefulness.
The secret stream scorns interval
Though the calendar shouts one from the wall ;
The spirit has no last days ;
And death is no more dead than this
Flower-haunted haze.

A PATROL

How quietly the by-road turns away
Past the hall gates and their entwined display
Of honours from old time ; but here the pride
Of dandelions rises, either side,
With heraldry of newer gloss. The sun
It seems they stem from. These frank knights have won
By this year's spring campaign the borders here,
And timely for some tournament appear,
Where Nature's war is news : where we who pass
Are deeper struck with the victory of the grass
Than all we view elsewhere of steel-sharp might
Which blows the babe and nurse to atoms in the night.

Here then we work our way ; no forlorn-hope
Had better chance than we, whose charming scope

Lies in this track, these peaceful flowers, this brook,
And past the crumbling bridge the wide outlook
Of woodside, crow-plain, grange and crescent hill.
No enemy there ; halt we, and vaunt our skill.
Prepare the triumph, clemency divine,
Command the taken thorpes to rise and shine,
White willows play the music, zephyrs bear
Banners and colours through the tented air.

Here we can free such fancies, here review
The country troops, heifer and steer and ewe ;
Forage the grove where fishponds well concealed
To courteous monks and us fat carp shall yield,
And herbs enough, and at the mill no lack
Of flour for nothing, had we but a sack.
Stay, in this fleet stream we will dip our toes
Where the fish darts as if by springs he goes.
Upon the root-fringed dais I will intrigue
A stately kiss to publish our high league.
You will bestow it with a grace, your heart
Will crown this crowning action ; thus apart
Your love which wakes to every sunbeam, moth,
Blossom, brook-melody, yeoman on his path,
Will clasp my life into a deep safe fold
And there shall be no more to do, no growing old.

But the day wanes, and townward bends the track,
And still the day is ours ; our steps might tack
A hundred ways to find the nightingale
Where men had heard her spring by spring, and fail,
But here's the very music, that is the one

Unsought, surprising, heaven-sent ; we have won
The goddess May, and so says your thrilled touch.
I did not dream one world could give so much.

THE GIFT: FOR C.M.P.

WERE it my fortune, I would bring you
A gift beyond the common rate,
Which, as it is, I can but sing you
And that with harshness forced of late :
But yet, O gentlest, hear my song.

It was a masterpiece, that isle
Of voiceful grasses and gay flowers ;
All told, one eighth of one square mile,
About whose bounds and hawthorn bowers
The river and the millcut sang along.

The mill-wheel, cheerful drudge, would roll
And splash and drum, but the bright-eyed vole
Would never care for him, would swim
Across his racing waves, and slim
Sharp dace would watch in the quickest gush,
And forget-me-not and flag and rush
Would take up quarters there, boom as he might.

And on the other side the weir
Controlled with rickety gate and gear
Poured forth a waterfall of cool
Jade streams and pearl drops into a pool

Of wonder, wide and round and deep,
Beneath banks counted fearful steep,
Encopsed, and crowned with oaks of age,
Each gray atop, an Archimage,
But the midpool still was the haunt of laughing light.

From pool and milltail rippling clear
Two sister streams made innocent way,
With many a tiny cape and bay
And tunnelled verge where red fins lay,
To meet again : the swans came here
Where these two nymphal kin would kiss,
And my great gift's comprised in this :
The heart-shaped meadow clasped in their career.

That had you seen, as then it bloomed
Amid great trees green-lit or gloomed,
And pranked with blue and russet wings,
Or manna-white with fairy-rings,
And trilling still with finch or lark
Or water-sonnet, or strong work
Descanting from the morning mill,
Or evening voices light and shrill
Of us assembled playing there,
You would much like the gift I bear
And make the colourless words look fair
With your resource of love, and love's all-seeing skill.

TIMBER

IN the avenues of yesterday
A tree might have a thing to say.
  Horsemen then heard
  From the branches a word
That sent them serious on their way.

A tree, — a beam, a box, a crutch,
Costing so little or so much ;
  Wainscot or stair,
  Barge, baby's chair,
A pier, a flute, a mill, a hutch.

That tree uprooted lying there
Will make such things with knack and care,
  Unless you hear
  From its boughs too clear
The word that has whitened the traveller's hair.

TO TEISE, A STREAM IN KENT

WATERSPRITE whose voice and look
Unique and multitudinous took
My childish fancy, at first glance
How clear the difference of your dance.
I could no more confuse your style
With Beult who flowed in the next green mile
Than take our smith or carrier for
Our saddler. Now, one plaudit more
For you, my strange familiar friend
And one deep prayer. May no man end
With short-seen plan or powerful greed
The centuries of your joy ; may reed,

Osier, pollard, alder, thorn
And oak defend you night and morn,
And cattle in your lily-pool
With sad stare shame away misrule.
May kingfishers like flames attack
Dullness and send him wiser back,
Squadrons of gem-eyed hobby-horses
Whirr round his iron-minded forces ;
And do you then, gentle stream,
Assume your wintriest wild extreme,
And (as I have known amazed) pour down
Among your goblin willows brown
Deep-dooming floods and foaming flocks
Of whirlwaves till the midnight rocks
With what you say to those who dare
Affront you with some coarse affair.

TRIUMPH OF AUTUMN

I SEE your signal, and the lands have seen,
And are prepared. Your hour, your fortune. Ride
More boldly then where none can intervene,
Not now in some pale bough or low mist hide.
With conquest occupy your splendid scene,
Throng the fantastic tourneyings of your pride.
Your hour, your fortune. Undisguise your will
And try your genius, king, from bannered grove to golden
hill.

Vast is the triumph which at your behest
Will blaze abroad. The sun himself shall stride

With clanging pomp, bronze east to rubied west,
The moon sway wine-flushed after, lion-eyed
Star-companies form, tree-columns of glittering crest
Uphold their rank in blue air, strong and wide
Rivers go wheeling through enormous plains,
Forests assume the purple, harvests roll their rumbling wains.

Meanwhile let no one whisper time's plain fact,
Or hint an embered ending. Leaves that sighed
In falling syllabled no wrath. The stacked
And vatted yield of the year has not denied
This cloth of gold. The church clock told exact
Moment on moment gone, but only plied
His task in the general show and with gilt hand
Paid compliment, meant nothing but a child may understand.

Who cannot now be glad with even the least
Of the pageant? Here the pear tree warped and dried,
There cob suspected barren, brings brave feast,
Bright apples lantern the earlier eventide.
With elder, hop, crab, blackberry, sloe increased
To swell your fame each straggling hedge has tried,
Great season; sunflowers clamber atop each fence,
Flaring salute, each aster like his master beams immense.

These in the margin of the world-wide page
Whereof you paint the midst, these orbed and pied
Delay the eye that you would wholly engage
With your own sanguine colours. Light airs glide

About your streamered car, your travelling cage.
They were but perfume wafting, and they died.
But some tell me they hear them gathering power
Until with ocean voice they sound the extinction of your
hour.

FOR THE COUNTRY LIFE

No sunbeam clearer
Than through our garret window ever leapt ;
The pearmain blossomed
Waiting for us who lightly slept
And often in our stockings crept

Into the scent of the morning,
The mist before the boundless day ;
Just for the fun we filled a bucket
In that white well whose springs allay
Us on our way

To join great hearts through thicker mist of battle,
Chaos of wills ; the smoke will yield.
The thing is only
For us to bring to the wise ones in the field
The strength so early revealed :

And with those sunbeams,
Those swallows under the eaves, and din
Of cockerels and larks and cuckoos
Let the battle for men begin,
And I think we shall win.

A PROSPECT OF SWANS

WALKING the river way to change our note
From the hard season and from harder care,
Marvelling we found the swans,
The swans on sullen swollen dykes afloat
Or moored on tussocks, a full company there,
White breasts and necks, advance and poise and stir
Filling the scene, while rays of steel and bronze
From the far dying sun touched the dead reeds.

So easy was the manner of each one,
So sure and wise the course of all their needs,
So free their unity, in that level sun
And floodland tipped with sedge and osiery,
It might have been where man was yet to be,
Some mere where none but swans were ever kings,
Where gulls might hunt, a wide flight in from sea,
And page-like small birds come : all innocent wings.

O picture of some first divine intent,
O young world which perhaps was modelled thus,
Where even hard winter meant
No disproportion, hopeless hungers none,
And set no task which could not well be done.
Now this primeval pattern gleamed at us
Right near the town's black smoke-towers and the roar
Of trains bearing the sons of man to war.

A CHURCH

FAR over cornfields to the rim of hills
With scarcely any house the church tower stares ;
Past trees as tall and great
Juts out its stony head.

Its kingdom is the farm, the farmer's lane
Its wheelworn churchway from the lonely road,
The farmer's house and barn
Its neighbours, others none.

The castle once stood close, the unhonoured mound
Stands yet yon side the moat where roach make rings,
Wilderness mad, a ghost
At noon and no one cares.

What churl devised this manor for old God ?
He had some scope of mind, rough as he was,
First reckoning God should have
A roomy house enough,

Something between a castle and a cave,
Indeed an immense byre and barn therewith,
For that earth-lord to pace
And thence watch out afield

Triumphant in his seasons and their stride.
With bull-like heads of stone the walls announce
His genius ; tempest breaks
Hence as his bellowing laugh.

About his doors he has his littered yard,
And quite forgets the use of these flung by,
Old implements of bones,
But will not have them moved.

Should you not find him manifest all hours there,
Maybe you met him big in the nettly lane,
Master of the endless world
Of clod, claw, root and man.

ON A JOURNEY, 1943

THE scythesman and the thatcher are not dead,
Or else their ghosts are walking with a will ;
Old England's farms are shrewdly husbanded,
And up from all the hamlets jumps old skill ;
I doubt not we shall have the land we love
And its ancestral faith and annual round
Flourishing by tried craftsmanship inwove
With modern science, in one purpose bound.
Therewith the church and country school can please
The spirit as they once did, daily shown
Famous as formerly among the trees
And ricks and barns, as from no fancy grown
But from the earth, and yielding flowers and fruits
To crown the rest of our robust pursuits.

THE ORNAMENTAL WATER

LIMNED in the lake the rosy portraiture
Of the great house on the rise through reed and bough
Seems still to announce that times are as they were,
Though no bright group descends the terrace now ;
The boat mud-foundered, the dry sluice allow
There's no youth coming home with joy this year,
The arbour's rankness hopes for no sweet vow
Sighed out as once within its shelter dear.

Weed-woven the shallowing pool, once pleasure's pride,
Returns to ancient use, the cattle's drink ;
The fallen oak-leaves and pale bubbles glide
Over their clear-kept haven at the brink ;
The bubbles make sharp stars run over the bed
Of silver sand, brave meteors — sudden-dead.

THE NAMELESS STREAM

I WONDER not the Poets love the brooks
And throughout life seek their society ;
I think there's scarcely one of their rich books
But has its stream that runs there merrily,
And plays as young as when their lives were new,
As musical as first it bade them hear,
Forget-me-nots in the banks as tender blue
As when their child loves chose them without fear.

Of all things young the reverence is not hard ;
It goes through nature, its own beauty smiles
Wherever life sets forth with brows unscarred
Singing its journey to enchanted isles.

Of all things young the brooks are not loved least,
So sparkling from their birth and dancing so ;
Their happy solitude has never ceased
To call the wise to wander where they flow.

Now in the bluebell wood in cool clefts poured
They brim their ivy-tangled pools and now
Wind into shallows parting pasture sward
And much they please the sun-teased horse and cow,
And spread white sands, and build up pebbly lairs
For loach and bullhead, while the flitting wren
Comes to live with them, and the kingfishers ;
And labourers bless them, and poetic men.

A COUNTRY CHARACTER

Homo Unius Libri

" LORD, how enchanting is the flow
Of words from that pure fountain,
Thy Book, to me.
How do I waken
On a sudden refreshed, my eyes empowered,
From the slumber that bound me,
When (at some wish of Thine)
Thy words, in sentence unforgettable,
Start forth in my path.
I find Thee apt,
And am assured by many histories
That if I use these words aright
I need not fall from the wild old horse
Who bears the name My Life.

So will he shy at fluttered papers, glimmering garments,
Or huge vans bumping past,
Sometimes I scarcely hold him,
And the torrent of tribulation roars ahead ;
But in this extremity
I hear the words, and he does :
' Lord, who shall dwell in thy tabernacle,
And who shall rest upon thy holy hill ?
Even he that leadeth an uncorrupt life.'
So will he go on gently.

Were the black thunder, as often has been,
To roll from ridge to ridge, hills turning waves,
And lightning mow through snake-grass rain about us,
This would not find me much in the frown ;
For out of the gloom should arise
A bower as of blossomed hawthorns, twined to let
No malice through, but every blossom a writing
Wreathed well, breathed sweeter than the winds of spring.

' Where thou goest, I will go,'
' I will come to you.'
' My peace I leave with you.'

Would that I had had money,
Not for my lavishing on luxuries,
Though with my savings I can always call
For my cup of ale, my ounce of bird's-eye, —
' I am as glad of Thy word
As in all manner of riches.'
If I had money I would set
Tall stones at every place where I was filled

With immediate admiration at the grace
Of Thy own speech, and this old skirring horse
Seemed too in his manner to read and mark the same,
Inscriptions to his eye, and music to his mind.
We have stood as sculptures, bright in a chancel sunrise.
The land should be full of these stones,
And Thy words over against them,
High as steeples, for ever.

Maybe it will be enough for a poor man
To trudge about two counties,
Painting on barn end, smithy wall and stile
With firm-drawn hand and finger pointing,
'The Kingdom of Heaven is at hand.
The Kingdom of Heaven is at hand.' "

DOVEDALE ON A SPRING DAY

APPROACH we then this classic ground :
More gentle name was never found
By chance, nor more of picturing sound
To tell the spirit of the scene ;
Be Dovedale ours this April day,
This April day that sheen or gray
May whip the wavelets into spray
Or flood with sun the margent green.

For all that wild work on the height
And driven clouds hailstone-gray, and fight
Of venturers on the ridge, delight
Is April's way and Dovedale's mind ;

These chasms and spikes that might elsewhere
Be monsters, horror's host, despair
In effigy, through this favouring air
Are hanging silks with dreams designed.

From those rich kingcups at the foot
Of soaring rock whence yew trees shoot
Up to the flashing swift pursuit
Of cloud on cloud where stone cuts sky,
It might be peril's deadliest hold ;
The wheeling rooks are much too bold,
To build there ? but the trees unfold
In tenderest green a sweet reply.

And see this stream that marches strong
With urgent and invincible song,
In myriad spearheads hurled along,
Assailing, sallying, arrowing miles ;
Immensely as his lordship roars,
He rides but into Oberon's wars,
Forget-me-not from both his shores
Watches his wrath with blue-eyed smiles.

Or is he so placated ? fear
And awe and doom are waiting here
Above the rock-browed shag-haired weir —
Stare not too long in these strange deeps.
Uncertain deep, they lead adown,
Their glassy languor masks some frown,
They house the ghost that means to drown —
Such sleeping water never sleeps.

As though the winter torrent lay
In ambush here this charming day
And still would whirl white limbs away,
    And count its undiscovered dead :
Yet let not snaky roots seem claws
Nor shelving pits have murdering maws, —
And from that stare which overawes,
    Look, the light stream himself is fled !

So those two anglers who might be
Walton and Cotton by a tree
Lay down their rods and leave trout free
    To quest up-stream, while they recall
Kind vanished days, or trace a scheme
Of prospering peace, utopian dream,
Which the better genius of the stream
    Sings to their hearts, this day in thrall.

And singing with him song perchance
Ancient as his, half walk, half dance
Sweet groups of young folk in romance,
    Their April twinkling in true eyes ;
The water-ouzel with white breast
Counts them familiar as the rest
Of Dovedale, where all good things nest,
    And by them lights, and seeks, and plies.

From abbot's-kitchen caves aloft
(I thought none lived there) cobweb-soft
A mystery grows, the winds up-waft
    The smoke of an enchanter's fire ;

But that enchanter proves no more
Than the boys' fancy who explore
His threshold, study and corridor,
    And gnome-like dart about his spire.

We here in grace have gladly passed
Beyond the world, behind us cast
Its tumult ; for that Titan blast
    Which makes the cawing rooks unheard
Is this dream's own, and we float on
In dream-time, love and nature one,
Hand folding hand, as flower and sun,
    And wave and stone, and song and word.

THOUGHTS OF THOMAS HARDY

" ARE you looking for someone, you who come pattering
Along this empty corridor, dead leaf, to my door,
And before I had noticed that leaves were now dying ? "

" No, nobody ; but the way was open.
The wind blew that way.
There was no other way.
And why your question ? "

" O, I felt I saw someone with forehead bent downward
At the sound of your coming,
And he in that sound
Looked aware of a vaster threne of decline,
And considering a law of all life.
Yet he lingered, one lovingly regarding
Your particular fate and experience, poor leaf."

GIBBON: IN THE MARGIN

WHAT would I give to have been
With Gibbon when first in great preview
While the barefooted friars were chanting their vespers
He gained his entire scene
Of imperial passions, contentions, illusions,
And out of them simply drew
The future's picture, man at last
Grown safe, schooled out of his perilous past?

What would I give to be
With some new Gibbon when all his thought
Over nations in throes and the springs of their quarrels
Perceives on a sudden the key
To the riddle, and comes to the multitude speaking
In honour and welcome? New-wrought
His engine of peace, I see him strong,
And the world amazed it had waited so long.

TO THE MEMORY OF COLERIDGE

MOONLIGHT and water mist
Like visions from your Ballad haunt the night,
And constellations burn above dark towers.
Alone at length
I come to you, my friend from boyhood hours,
My Grecian, test of truth and tower of strength,
With great desire to tell you how your light
Streams from your cottage window, blow wind as it list.

Time's face with shadows red
Of doubt and error, rage and grudge lours still.
I turn to you, Ulysses of your day
Whose view comprised
So many times and nations, whose survey
Made seers of those who heard you : thence advised
I catch beyond the transient chaos shrill
The music of a mind which yet moves well ahead.

Your faith, which casual wit
Follows not far, compact of lore and love,
Of near or distant image, gleams and yields
A promise now ;
And through the moonlight, in our towns and fields,
Yearn the immortals. Once again the vow
Is made to them, pagan and Christian move
For the soul's health, and as in your wide world unite.

At this you frown ; I hide
My face a moment, if therein I err,
And am content to stay where last you pointed —
These English shrines
Beneath high elms best house the Lord's anointed,
And the Triune you loved there loveliest shines.
In fields you said that natural altars were,
But for the perfect godhead stood at Herbert's side.

Had our time-tracks combined,
Much had I moved you to that gracious gift,
Which crowned the rest ; you had raised more dream-towers with
Your far-sweet song ;

You whose young fairy-secret is my myth,
Whose pilotage is safe through seas of wrong,
Whose years of joy and pain finally lift
Over the age the timeless house of singing mind.

LASCELLES ABERCROMBIE

It was not mine to know your younger strength,
But from your words I caught some charming sense
Of the glad lyrist now in orchards walking,
Now on high moors, and always friend of morning,
Curious and happy in the rural round.
Great was your wisdom in all kinds of learning,
As though you could have lectured to Longinus,
Or taken a flail with Clare, or sailed with Shelley,
And tuned Æolian harps or mended millwheels,
Or founded bells or run a raree-show.
Modesty never beaten ruled your talk
Of that great art which through all usual tasks
Lived in you ; serious-sweet you guarded that
From casual comment and from personal aim,
Still meditating what the masters wrote
And building temples to the Muse apart.
I feared not your untimely vanishing,
I thought you had before you still a calm
Chaucerian age, and every witty glance,
Clear recollection, dry reflection proved it.
So lost ! yet the brief season of our meetings
Is on my life most graciously inscribed.

ONE KIND OF ARTIST

RAINBOWS on flying foam, glitterings of high-sunned cloud,
Anthems of west wind tuning the reeds and fled away,
Such were his works. They could not hold the crowd,
And we who wished him luck felt some dismay.

Such evident gift of vision, such sense of expression as well,
Such bliss in the making of art's illusion this man had ;
Beauty and mystery his ! but each bloom fell
Almost as each bloom came, so glad, so sad.

Often companions delayed him, privately counselling, " Strive
For more of permanence, founding, coherent thought as theme."
" Consider what keeps old Greek plays alive."
" Mankind needs steady light, not fitful gleam."

Nodding he listened, assented and even gave promise or pledge.
Bright was his look as he came next time with his best,
Which still flew past like goldfinches over a hedge
Or lingered as long as gold clouds in the west.

THE TWO BOOKS

Come tell me : of these two books lying here,
Which most moves heart and mind to tenderness,
The one approaching its three-hundredth year,
The other a recruit fresh from the press ?
The one well honoured down the years, and still
Trusty to light our pathway, poise our view,
And this as yet uncrowned, which may fulfil
As great a task through centuries strange and new ?
In both you find one nature, one appeal,
And that antiquity and this young birth
Share the same glory, equally reveal
Man in his wisest, luckiest hours on earth.
Man the inventive with his ceaseless power
Of shaping engine, fabric, instrument,
Never wrought better than in the early hour
Which gave him books ; and to his short span lent
Almost eternity, to his local speech
Almost unbounded range. Thus from the tomb
Unseen romancers charm, apostles teach,
The white truths conquer and the kind loves bloom.
A world so opens on us by this key,
We may not count its continents ; we may glide
Over a myriad-times extended sea
And land of life abundant, time denied.
And this, like roses in the year's decline,
This blest invention grows much sweeter now,
And while the rest is shadow this will shine,
Invincible amid great overthrow ;
So speak and mean these two books lying here,
And differing as may be, alike grow dear.

THE FLORILEGIUM

An Ancient Anthologist Speaks

"FROM Helicon's unfading hill
With these my flowers I come to fill
The minds of men who else might miss
Their heavenly honey, truth and bliss ;
Such flowers as mine, let frankness say,
Sprang not for young Proserpina
In Enna, and this rare sweet store
I bring to every wise man's door,
I bring the coronals I wove
From all that deck time's favourite grove,
And you who take the gift in bloom
Will find Parnassus in your room.

And this I cannot doubt your knowing :
My basket filled to overflowing
Contains no flower which by its tempting hue
Or magic breath might do
An injury to the soul of truth
Or displease age, or cozen youth.
Out of the holy woodland fed with dews
Sprinkled by every gracious Muse
My amaranths diffuse
Only a living and life-giving air,
The quintessence of all sweet things that ever were.
It cost some toil to win them,
But such the pleasure in them,
Toil was blessing ;
Heaven smiled on the ways I passed
And with a prayer I culled the last

Sentence divine, new heavens expressing.
Where virtue's lily queened it there came I,
And lilies give you now which do not die ;
Where the sun-loving kinds arose to quell
The weed of error, those I sought as well.

Look now on my good pages,
Remark what themes provide them and what men.
See at the first, clear ABSTINENCE engages
Your ready spirit ; each a golden pen,
Ovid and *Owen* meeting here agree
That Abstinence is truly luxury.
Turn to the end of the whole where in much clear
Display of numbers, it will well appear
What WIVES should be, and why to be held dear,
Of which grave *Seneca* decides :
' Husbands, seek beauty in your brides,
Not in the outward but the inward part,
Their constancy and gentleness of heart.'
Sprang not that flower, one touch of which can smooth
A sea of troubles, from the ground of truth ?
My garden blooms, portal to postern so,
With healthful herbs, and yet a gallant show,
Vernal, eternal, tinct with vital gold,
And music in them ; poets new and old,
Chorus of morning stars ! by godlike powers
Have fashioned flowers of songs and songs of flowers.
Here banquet then, exhilarate every vein
From these our cordials, this my goblet drain
And wiser be ; if one that's sensual sneer,
I see him later doubt, he should have made one here.

With Virgil walk in these elysian fields,
Accept what Mantuan, what Boëthius yields.

Such treasure has this danger, it may seem
Too much for mortals. Fear not. Range and deem
One flower the pride of all : That which will shine
In season due a perfect high design,
A crown-imperial, is no sudden birth,
But from a slow increase acquires its worth,
Must from its opening labour to attain,
And gather grace from wind and sun and rain."

A PAINTED WINDOW

Stored Underground for the Period of War

FIGURED in gray and brown
By some mynheer, whole worlds ago,
Conveyed for safety down
(Such safety, no one seems to know
Where it reclines to-day) —

Recall its panelled scenes
In the wry taste of other times,
Its angels, kings and queens,
Its banquets, turrets, brawls and crimes, —
All snugly stowed away.

The Deadly Sins stood there
Full length and flourished in their lust,
Were blithe and debonair :

But the end was certain, sterve they must
For all their antic hay.

Why then were careful brows
Wrinkled to keep these ne'er-do-wells
Secure ? Shall future vows
Arise to them, and honour of bells,
When they come forth one day ?

Perhaps in a final war
The purge of Vice (men felt) would cut
Such forms from living lore.
Millennium might not trace them, but
That these had leave to stay.

Avarice, Anger and you,
Salacious, hoggish, except for this,
You and the whole of the crew
Must have perished in the last abyss.
Reprieved ! come home next May.

TRAVELLERS, 193-

BRIGHT insolent winds assail the shores
Of northern France, and the crested waves
Tilt at the miles of sands and shingles
Where as yet no public misbehaves.

Pale painters get a trifle busy
On the shut kiosks and blank cafés,
But as yet there's more suspicion than hurry
And the wind will pound yet several days.

Wild scampering sunbeams show the city
  Is clamorous red and silver blue,
And straight-lined fortifications yield
  Part shelter, whence that coloured view.

Strong-elbowed and with wondrous beard,
  Whose statue's this ? read who it is, Clare ;
Who, I'll forget inside ten minutes,
  And I'll not forget you reading it there.

I wonder, I, the older traveller,
  What you and John are taking back, —
Nothing maybe of my perceptions ;
  A different series, another tack.

The wind may sing his sea-song later
  In your review as he will in mine,
The coast of England gloom and glitter
  To you as to me : so the moment shine,

It will be enough, for watching you meeting
  With foreheads smooth this sharp clean day,
I feel at once deep joy and trouble,
  And winds blowing each a separate way.

A REMEMBRANCE

SOME tune or phrase, some scene or face,
  Some hidden precious thing
Is given to each, and starts a grace,
  Makes the day sing.

The young self of a friend long gone
  Up roads not mine still calls,
When least expected ; wings me on,
  Dares the blank walls.

And how should he, of all, resume
  So much the sudden song ?
For nothing now connects our doom,
  Each thinks the other wrong.

Yet for my luck let him remain
  That speedy lawless boy,
Through slush and gale and sleet and rain
  Whistling his joy ;

Who by the crinkling run of the brook
  And blue bird's herald flight
Stood a wild elf-boy with far look
  Of Spring's delight.

OCTOGENARIAN

" OLD we shall find him ; eighty years
Is not so young." These private fears
After long absence almost bore
Our steps beyond his by-street door.

We found him old : himself, he inveighed
Against such age, which mischief made
The daily round, in war-time too,
Rather too much for him to do.

Four hundred thousand men had he
  Preparing for the kill.
Four hundred thousand men there lay,
The Big Battalions blessed the day ;
What forest of standards might dismay
  Tigranes in his splendour ?

As he scanned the troops and the armament
  That caught the eye of the sun,
In faith he looked on the top of the world
  And a chief if there ever was one.
His black and silky beard just so,
His clever chin, his smooth white brow,
His eye of jet with fires aglow
  To burn through the walled town.

But here are the scouts come steaming in
  And spur for the General's tent,
And the boyish officer cannot but grin
  As he shadows the day's event :
" They are marching, Sir, they are heading for here,
The Romans, fourteen thousand clear."
And fourteen thousand begin to appear
  In the huge green plain's extent.

The Triton stares at the minnows,
  " They are rather too many," says he,
" For an embassy, rather too few for a fight."
  The army catches his glee.
" He has said it," observe the General Staff,
Snatching last mouthfuls of pilaff,

On the rich and unknown fruits up-piled
  Along the market lanes,
And like yourself you looked and smiled,
  So high above the plains.
But higher yet was in the place,
  That overwhelming dome
Or nave or tower, of each the trace,
  This people's haunt and home.
A work so vast, its upper range
  Vanished in sparkling haze,
And coloured, like a country grange,
  Gold-browns and bluebell grays.
A work of wonder, yet to these
  Who crowded streets and shops
It seemed not so, nor the silvering trees
  That next it set their tops
Anigh the dragons of its first storey.
  To us the like showed never,
High terror drank we in and glory
  Of genius the upheaver.
But what compulsion, what decoy
  Must hurry us from the hall
Where life seemed all a summer joy
  Within a sacred wall?
A word or two with the busy folk
  Might have made us of their kind,
But as it chanced we neither spoke,
  And the town soon lay behind,
To live its life beneath its tower,
  So I suppose, as long
As that dream-builder counts an hour
  Who himself was one of the throng.

NATURE AND THE LOST

" Now all are gone, and I a moment pause,
And would for a long age be restful,
Since that most gifted and enquiring brood
Has vanished, the great promise ended
After a history stranger than their own conjectures.
I am past tears, which they once dreamed I wept
Even for one of their master-spirits leaving
His body to my clays and weeds and darkness.

The child was ever a problem, the lovely eye
Inclined to a glitter of pride, the capable hand
Willing to rend and work out means of rending.
From that divine brow sprang
Fevers for all my others, — no loss counted
Compared with the full exploit of those strong thoughts.

Those now enacted have but quelled each other ;
Analysis of good and evil stops.
Lear and Lear's shadow leave their shattered stage,
Nothing has come of nothing, as he mentioned.
The builder and unbuilder both cease work.
Yet I had fancied, from scraps of talk somewhile,
A wiser way had brought them safe towards joy
And a planetary peace where none need cease.

One knows not one's own children,
They come as strangers,
They form and choose as we did not foretell.
The best may not be soundest.

Now these are gone, and I would plead some stay
Of the next gendering, but my prayer falls dull,

For I am fruitful unto fate each hour,
And the new seed will swiftly march
Over the waiting world : then, may its will
Be second to its sense, its genius less
Than its receptiveness, its lore of self
No more than what these have who yet surround me
Answering the sun with song, and storm with patience."

THE LOST NAME

No ship perhaps again will ever bear
That fatal name
Which at the christening challenged everywhere
Seafaring fame.

But now we see calamity so vast,
Multiplied so
That time may quite forget that wreck of the past,
— No one would know.

And under her gray name a proud new ship
May yet advance,
Thronged with young faces brilliant for the trip :
God guard the dance !

AIRCRAFT

OVER the streams and roofs the moon rides high :
Not the white moon alone.
Aircraft superbly flown
With throbbing songs of venture fill the sky.

And these now earthward in their main intent
May not be found so, soon.
Minded beyond the moon,
Man will enlarge his winged experiment.

For this the moon seems not at all to care ;
With her accustomed mien,
As though man had not been,
She moves on heaven's old highway, unaware.

THE BOY ON LEAVE

So you have chosen, saying little, knowing
That surface paths are counted easier going,
That other wars make quicker, gaudier showing ;
But here you are, an hour.
You walk the hillside clad
In your mind's peace ; you make us glad ;
You ask the name of stone or flower,
And it might seem that twinkling roof or tower
Was your objective, this lithe hill-beck flowing
Your water-world, these sheepfolds your blockade.

Young scientist of war ! and surely skilled
In greater knowledge since you so proceeded —
But in strange channels needed
You pass from us, and passing take each field,
Each barn and copse, the whole wide landscape blue.
These highways, headlands all belong to you.
Your eyes that soon in crampt metallic dive
Must see hard, swift and bleak if any will survive,

Enfold the slow-bloomed scenes. The brief hour flies.
Henceforth I see them chiefly mirrored in your eyes.

THE VICTOR

O LIGHTENING love that makes drab lanes
Bright avenues to joy's high way,
And forth from black-souled hurricanes
Conjures glad day !

O limitless love that he and she
Find winged for worlds in one embrace ;
That under one small roof or tree
Commands all space !

O living love in whose great birth
Death counts for nothing, proved a lie,
Still blaze and blossom through old earth,
And sea and sky.

LOVELIGHT

SUCH light calm moonrise never gave,
Nor dawn clear-issuing wave on wave :
No flower pale-gold from dell or sill
Looked forth so blest, none ever will.
Much had he lived for happy grace
In heaven and earth, but her young face
Charmed into one all else he knew,
And bloomed unknown enchantment too,

With smiling chaste extreme content
Regarding him that over leant,
While some freed fountain of delight
Played beauty ripple-fresh and bright ;
Which viewing, how he joyed, how trembled lest the the dream take flight,
But still she lay in's arms, and still her countenance sang with light.

THE FINE NATURE

THIS fine nature clear
Goes as a stream through brake and pasture,
Questioning not, disdaining none,
Fair friend alike of shade and sun.
We happening near
Are offered, without any rumour or fear,
A gentleness, a strength, the way
That first was meant the heart of man
Should go when meeting the unsolved hours,
And so few can,
But this one counts the age in flowers :
So fragrance, colour, jewel, song
Attend along.

How great the miracle I find,
While all is zoned with thunder-smoke,
In such a constant mind, —
Which, serious-playful as the brook,
And with like gift of beauty won
From stem or stone, from walk or run,
Amid my meadows cannot be
But ever kind and ever free.

FULFILMENT

FULFILMENT is a puzzling goddess,
And though her jewelled shrine
Is so magnetic, we may tarry
And ask, Is she divine ?

But if the answer be, No question,
Still let us spend our gift
Of time on pilgrimage together,
And watch the lazy drift

Of autumn leaves in casual currents
Towards the new-found weir,
And count the unimpassioned willows
And dreamless palings here ;

And pass the corporal with his sweetheart,
And happily dissent
Over the hue poured in the waters
From the modern tenement

Which ventures nearly to our river ;
Its blue-frocked children play
Carelessly there where Nature played with
Solitude yesterday.

And I, concerned to see the picture,
Suspect Fulfilment wins ;
Wherever we had forecast her chapel,
Here her reign begins.

There was a hope — but I have forgotten,
For now is hope fulfilled ;
And, watching your bright brow this moment,
I have no house to build.

THE FLOWERS

THEY fade then ; other flowers have faded,
And these were flowers.
Had I been watching closer or less jaded,
They should have lived yet some sweet hours.

But in their spent bloom I discover
Not care alone,
But what live truth it is to be your lover,
And know you make my course your own.

Bringer of flowers ! and friend of failings,
Young and brave love,
I count these wraiths as my own unavailings,
And yet my thoughts towards you in glory move.

THE WATERFALL

I HAUNT a waterfall
Not so tall
Measured by mapcraft, but to me
None is there through this world to see
From mightiest peak or blue rock wall
Like this fair fall.

I haunt a waterfall, —
    So I call
These flowing shining locks set free
Whereamid a spirit of Nature she
With eyes of love looks forth to enthral ;
    Whom fair and fair befall.

THE HAPPIEST

How surpassingly happy the musician
On whose mind is suddenly alighted
The new, right, flame-clear, brook-cool melody !
To hear it first of all the world
That will wonder where in all the world
This natural beauty so long dallied,
Being eternal, being perfect.

Glad may he be, the exile, to whose room
A child ghost comes, all brilliant,
The pearl, the rosebud,
The watching, silent, wondering one,
But that encounter cannot stay ;
Happier shall I call the soldier
Who, cleansed anon from the hobs of hell,
And miraculously delivered,
Sees his home, finds his old cap
Hung where he hung it,
The clover-scent filling the yard, the carrier's cart
    just passing.

Happier still than those the musician
To whom in his room above the pompous boulevard

And umbrellas hurrying in the gray shower
The fine music flies, eager to be enthralled.
And still I call one happier
Whose life receives
The air that ever was, and never was —
The announcement of unfaltering love.

TIME TOGETHER

WHEN you are by, I think of time as boys
Set forth on brave excursions in the spring,
Which opens the green landscape and long hours ;
I am all contentment, never a presage lours
On my delicious pastures ; the blue ring
Of heaven perhaps I mark, beyond my joys ;
But that's too far for fear ; if that be all,
Why, I can say there's room, no fence obtrudes nor wall.

Such is your well-tuned, wild-flowered, world-bright
grace,
Giving me sense of wide free ways, so free
And wide that I count nothing of time and space,
But think these present gifts will ever be ;
Childlike the bliss, and childlike too dismayed
I find the moment come which ends our endless glade.

AMONG ALL THESE

GRACES in the air, or from earth or wave
Have taken me, wooed me along,
And made my memory a happy slave,
Set the range of my saying or song.

With the storm on the far hills rushing down
  In a passion of dark and bright,
Or the poplars silvery-showery blown,
  I have counted the time delight.

The sudden seraphical faultless host
  Of bell-flowers where none pass,
The blue sea frilling the sleepy coast,
  The gale in the sorrelled grass,

The budding willow by the pond, the cloud
  Soft-flaming past the mountain wall,
Have made me cheer and challenge aloud ;
  And among these graces all

Supremacy dwells with her who blooms,
  And glitters, who hastens or delays,
Much as nature bids with rays or glooms,
  And will not blame my praise ;

Whether she on the sea-cliff seize
  The round world with her joy,
And by the twisted thorny trees
  In the wild sun play the boy,

Or in deeper mood by the fire we share
  Gaze down and silent remain,
Her musing eyes hidden in her hair
  Bright-falling like springtide rain.

CLAIRE'S BIRTHDAY IN 1940

THIS is your day, but can this be your year ?
What likeness bears this angry turbid stream
Of months with one hoarse theme
To your long love of life and welcome clear
For all that wars not, growing in its place, —
What has this curse to do with your embrace ?

Yet for your birthday let us make our rhyme,
Wishing old Chaucer near to do it right,
Who would have hailed your light
And sent your legend far beyond a time
Of passions armed with horror and hell-pride,
And shown your fineness as the future's bride.

Royally would he have sung, since he had skill
In portraiture of ladies' loveliness,
What I can only bless :
The happy beauty dawning brighter still
Each day from noble forehead, fearless eyes,
Lips where with wit deep understanding vies.

THE SPRING GALE

SOUND, sound, immortal Tempest, through the dark,
Set a pent heart, a captive wild-bird free,
For I have One who passes every mark
To run and rise and round the world with thee.
And she is timeless, unenslaved is she,

The spring's great impulse all the year indwelling
In her warm breast, and tirelessly excelling
The dust of dry extinction : Sound in tree
And arch and reed, for there will my Love be,
Of all the Venus and the vital spark ;
And, herald, conqueror, epitome
Of sharp and sweet begetment, only agree
That thou as she art gentle ; dawn shall hark
With me to your one song from the heaven-beseeching lark.

ONE AMONG THE ROSES

WHILE by the rosebed gay you stood, and revelled in the multitude
Of blooms with unfamiliar names, and tints and folds new-found, new-sweet,
We wondered much at the rich power which breeds so many and many a flower
Not like the myriads known before, and each one lovely and complete.

And while you touched the leaves and bowed your bright head there among the crowd,
Murmuring of roses you would have in the small garden of your dream,
I wondered much at the great grace which fashioned your clear rosy face,
After the myriads gone before, a beauty new and now supreme.

THOMASINE

No stranger yet no friendlier call
Ever did befall
Young clear-spoken Thomasine
On all the errands she had been
By chapel, covert, warren, hall
Than that vast evening floodlit far
With the sun gone down, so calm, so clear.

It was little enough, save there and then.
The moorcock crowed and called his hen
A distance off in a pool unseen
Of that quicksilver, that sharp green
Beyond the mill and weir,
All so clear,
All so secret ; again the cry
Climbing the miles and miles of sky.

Here some wood stacked, there a van,
A slated sty, a rusty can,
A notched millstone, a pumiced step,
A walnut tree and a bee-skep.
The miller's house, that stares at distant land.
She had him thenceforth in her hand ;
She knocked, he came ; it might have been planned ;
But her thought was up the stream —
That call in the reeds was all her theme.

" This I should read at once — forgive me ;
Child, come in, and kindly give me
A moment or two to think it over."
Thomasine, scan well your lover.

All past guesses, all your glancings,
Preferences and fragile advancings,
Flown with the last of the snowflakes, see you ?
But his plain business waits not — be you
Gone to your dad with the answer now.

Who shall determine how
She and he, thus met on a rarish
Journey into the bounds of the parish,
Meet and meet ? Life's many-roomed
Mansion has but one room for them now,
He would kiss her mantle's hem now,
Only now known ; and she has bloomed.

The afterglow, a wild-bird's voice,
A sound of sluices, could these make
A charm which lured her to her choice,
And gave her subtle strength to take
Like any witch ? I dare not screen
My thought from the chance that just this one
Reed-note from beyond the world else known
Woke a new song in sauntering Thomasine.

See, she comes, she dances it down
The furze-hill lane by the sandpit brown ;
She can count the way by grains of sand,
She knocks, and has him in her hand.
And he, straight worker, not the worst
Of heirs, not catching her at first,
Is now alive to her alive,
And blue night falls. The splashing rills

Over the deep-dropt penstocks dive,
The trout's leap trills
And the waters resound in a round.

" Finish the day, pack those away,
Those tiresome papers," — he complies,
And still she leads. " I hear you play."
The music challenges. While it dies,
She from some lovely distance cries
A note she learned ; he must obey.
Can this, she asks, be Thomasine ?
Can ever such dear love have been ?

They are talking trouble, along the street,
Talking Wicked, Indiscreet, —
Few will be pleased, but gods are pleased
When love comes flying for love once more.
Most forget, some never heard
That simple and mysterious word
That came to Thomasine, who knew.
Nature tried and found her true.
She told this to a friend, who smiled
Sadly at things so silly and wild.

The primrose here I'd happily bring
To peep with grace, the wren to sing ;
The thrush's egg I'd borrow to deck
This chronicle with a hue as pure
As it should have ; the royal swan's white neck
Should not the shining whiteness there one whit
    obscure.

" Love, I was nothing till you made me Me."
" And I was here alone, and here are We."
Thence in its strength their epithalamy.
The mirror gleams in the shades, the ancient house
Whispers of something known to the apple-boughs
Just by the window ; she, a thought alone,
Listens to all the night, comes, claims her own.
All the hosts of fear are nothing here,
Grudge and bad cheer
Overthrown.
He does her no wrong ; she wins him, she the flood
That bears him childlike, while he thinks his voyage good.

Day, and life ahead ;
Would it were mine to utter more
Than from some broken knowledge now was said,
And trace them in Time's wonder, shore on shore
Achieving ; only trust we this,
Under our harsh world wells such constant bliss.
Blessed it is, and when it upsprings through,
Its beauty assoils the worst that hate can do.
Blessed that sign of venture given, that chime
From solitude when reeds are green,
And answered as by Thomasine
Through the tangles of chance and time.

THE WINTER WALK

Now while the winter wind at last,
  As angered by delay,
Hurls all he has of shrewd or vast
  To pound the world to clay ;

While brown woods slant and sing his hymn
With roaring voice, and shed
Here droves of leaves and there a limb,
And look like witch-worked dead ;

I walk alone, and walking so
As ever find you there,
And talk with you, and boldly go
Through all this rush and tear

As if it were the calmest place
And moment, and as though
That sunshaft lit fair Nature's face
With all the flowers that blow.

And off it flies, and leaves the plain
In desolate dying need,
Wherefrom the shapes of summer's reign,
The latest born, recede.

Once more they humbly sink away,
Their little lives resigned
Might scarcely want this tempest day
To cut them from God's mind.

And I who pass much like the sere
And outcast leaves and straws
Must think on all that disappear
By these inclement laws ;

The more because my mind is bent
On brightest souls, on one

Who seemed for ever-living meant,
For an age of song and sun.

And you with me, well-loving long
That mortal, smiling sigh —
As sweet and sad as his best song —
" But even I shall die."

I have no thoughts, nor could have words,
Nor will I yet believe —
I look away to feeding herds
Who kindly might deceive.

Their honest heads, their lusty sides,
Their haltless pasturing claim
That, whatever airy demon rides,
They find the world the same ;

And look, those birds with perfect ease,
Proud-crested, not a care
From the black north unsteadies these :
They have all time to spare.

Fine-drawn illusion ! still my heart
Chills with the truth I know,
That all created joy must part
And the very brightest go :

A river wider than all sense
Of measure, whose skull-waves
Are all whom winter hustled hence,
Whose eddies are the graves

Of million millions, glorious grown,
  Then of no interest,
This river all too clearly known
  Comes flooding through the breast.

" O heart," I hear you say, and feel
  Your warm hand on my hand,
" Be peaceful, let the storm of steel
  Rush timely through the land

Without the cohort of your dreams,
  Unless such dreams as bring
Me to your arms ; your lethe-streams
  Will vanish at the spring."

They vanish now ; I hear no storm,
  I fear none ; you are spring,
The golden meadows western-warm
  Around us flower and sing,

And if eternal be, its light
  Is upon our now, our here,
While you cast Maydays on Time's night,
  My beautiful and dear.

GOD'S TIME

A GENTLER heaven steals over the hour,
    And at its pace I go
    And scan green things that grow
Beneath old hedge and ivy-bower.
Most gracious falls the silent hour.

Through the shut sky an eye of blue
    Twinkles upon the soul,
    Even as these weeds unroll
Their leaves aspiring, choice and new ;
Their greenness blesses, and that blue.

The round leaf, shield leaf, patterned spray
    All shine like love's first tears,
    And though no primrose peers,
Nor aconites, nor windflowers play,
I have their message through leaf and spray.

This may not be the hour I supposed
    When from the house I came
    Informed of a world aflame ;
That will have been an era closed,
Though endless as I then supposed.

O green leaves born in winter's heart,
    White ghosts of flowers to be,
    Come here so quietly,
And blossoming heaven's blue counterpart,
— I have lost my way, and found my heart.

AT A CATHEDRAL SERVICE

" The almond will soon be flowering," said she
With Nature's smile on her lip, in her eye,
" Though here there may be no almond tree,
But I feel it so." The New Year sky

Was shining on the Cathedral then,
" I hope the sun shines through the windows," she said,
And into matins we went once again,
In peace and love and thankfulness wed.

Through the windows tall and white the sun
Shone well, and his rays blest the simple hour,
Touched the cheeks of the children, and haloed one
White effigy, made the almond flower
In my Love's mood, while the trees in the wind
With light dancing branches beyond the glass
Seemed to have buds they dreamed to unbind,
To reach beyond months of steel and brass.

The voice of the prophet so often read
Was new again and the vision new,
And said to my depths what my dear had said ;
The singing of the boys resounded it too.
We wished that the world might all be won
By the chime and colour the moment wove,
The almond blossom of spirit, the sun
Of diviner fires, and eternal love.

THE END

Printed in Great Britain by R. & R. Clark, Limited, *Edinburgh*